Raquel y Joaquín

Cathy Camarena, M.Ed., and Gloria B. Ruff, M.Ed.

Consulting Editors

Lourdes Flores-Hanson, M.S.E., and Gloria Rosso-White

ABDO
Publishing Company

Published by ABDO Publishing Company, 4940 Viking Drive, Edina, Minnesota 55435.

Printed in the United States.

Credits
Curriculum Coordinator: Nancy Tuminelly
Cover and Interior Design and Production: Mighty Media
Child Photography: Steven Wewerka, Wewerka Photography
Photo Credits: AbleStock, Comstock, Eyewire Images, ShutterStock, Stockbyte

Library of Congress Cataloging-in-Publication Data

Camarena, Cathy, 1966-
    Raquel y Joaquín / Cathy Camarena, Gloria B. Ruff.
       p. cm. -- (Primeros sonidos)
    ISBN 1-59679-893-9 (hardcover)
    ISBN 1-59679-894-7 (paperback)
    1. Spanish language--Consonants--Juvenile literature. I. Ruff, Gloria B., 1971-
    II. Title. III. Series.
    PC4159.C3725 2006
    468.1'3--dc22
                                                                          2005056907

SandCastle™ books are created by a professional team of educators, reading specialists, and content developers around five essential components that include phonemic awareness, phonics, vocabulary, text comprehension, and fluency. All books are written, reviewed, and leveled for guided and early intervention reading, and designed for use in shared, guided, and independent reading and writing activities to support a balanced approach to literacy instruction.

Let Us Know

After reading the book, SandCastle would like you to tell us your stories about reading. What is your favorite page? Was there something hard that you needed help with? Share the ups and downs of learning to read. We want to hear from you! To get posted on the ABDO Publishing Company Web site, send us e-mail at:

sandcastle@abdopub.com

SandCastle Level: Beginning

Qq

ABCChDEFGH

IJKLLLMNÑOP

QRSTUVWXYZ

abcchdefgh

ijklllmnñop

qrstuvwxyz

Raquel

Joaquín

panqueque

queso

mariquita

querubín

15

quince

El está aquí.

El está aquí.

La está aquí.

Aquí está el .

Mira el número 15.

A Raquel y a Joaquín le gustan los panqueques.

Los panqueques
son grandes.

Los panqueques
están sabrosos.

Raquel y Joaquín comen quince panqueques.

¿Cuáles de estas cosas contienen **que/qui**?

15

Más palabras que contienen **que/qui**

chaqueta

mantequilla

quesadilla

500

quinientos

quiosco

About SandCastle™

A professional team of educators, reading specialists, and content developers created the SandCastle™ series to support young readers as they develop reading skills and strategies and increase their general knowledge. The SandCastle™ series has four levels that correspond to early literacy development in young children. The levels are provided to help teachers and parents select the appropriate books for young readers.

Emerging Readers
(no flags)

Beginning Readers
(1 flag)

Transitional Readers
(2 flags)

Fluent Readers
(3 flags)

These levels are meant only as a guide. All levels are subject to change.

To see a complete list of SandCastle™ books and other nonfiction titles from ABDO Publishing Company, visit **www.abdopub.com** or contact us at:
4940 Viking Drive, Edina, Minnesota 55435 • 1-800-800-1312 • fax: 1-952-831-1632